EUCHARISTIC PRAYER FOR MASSES
FOR VARIOUS NEEDS AND OCCASIONS

prepared by
International Commission on English in the Liturgy
A Joint Commission of Catholic Bishops' Conferences
WASHINGTON, D.C.   1994

THE LITURGICAL PRESS

Collegeville   Minnesota

Concordat cum originali:
Alan F. Detscher
Executive Director, Secretariat for the Liturgy

Published by authority of the Committee on the Liturgy of the National Conference of Catholic Bishops.

ACKNOWLEDGMENTS

Eucharistic Prayer for Masses for Various Needs and Occasions © 1994, International Committee on English in the Liturgy, Inc. All rights reserved.

Musical settings of the *Eucharistic Prayer for Masses for Various Needs and Occasions* © 1994, International Committee on English in the Liturgy, Inc. All rights reserved.

The reproduction of this translation in any form requires written permission of the International Committee on English in the Liturgy, in accordance with its policy on copyright and procedure.

International Commission on English in the Liturgy
1275 K Street, N.W., Suite 1202
Washington, D.C. 20005-4097 U.S.A.

Arrangement of this prayer as four separate prayers and adaptations of the musical settings to conform to the USA edition © 1995, United States Catholic Conference, 3211 Fourth Street, N.E., Washington, D.C. 20017.

Cover design by Ann Blattner

© 1996 by The Order of St. Benedict, Inc., Collegeville, Minnesota 56321. Printed in the United States of America.

ISBN 0-8146-2435-9

CONTENTS

FOREWORD

This booklet contains the ICEL interim translation of the text for the *Eucharistic Prayer for Masses for Various Needs and Occasions* which was approved by the National Conference of Catholic Bishops at its November 1994 meeting.

The Latin version of this prayer consists of one prayer with four thematic prefaces and corresponding sets of intercessions. For ease of use, the prayer has been printed as four separate prayers, as is already provided for in the *Ordinario de la Misa* in Spanish approved for use in the dioceses of the United States of America.

NATIONAL CONFERENCE OF CATHOLIC BISHOPS

UNITED STATES OF AMERICA

DECREE

The *Eucharistic Prayer for Masses for Various Needs and Occasions* was promulgated as the Latin typical edition of what was formerly known as the "Swiss Synod Eucharistic Prayer" by the decree of the Congregation for Divine Worship and the Discipline of the Sacraments of August 6, 1991 (Prot. CD 511/91).

The interim English translation of the *Eucharistic Prayer for Masses for Various Needs and Occasions* prepared by the International Commission on English in the Liturgy was approved by the Latin Rite members of the National Conference of Catholic Bishops on November 16, 1994. Subsequently, on May 9, 1995 (Prot. N. 92/95/L), Antonio Cardinal Javierre, Prefect of the Congregation for Divine Worship and the Discipline of the Sacraments, authorized the interim English translation of this eucharistic prayer for use in the liturgy until the new translation of the Roman Missal is confirmed.

On October 1, 1995, the *Eucharistic Prayer for Masses for Various Needs and Occasions* may be published and used in the liturgy until such time as the definitive translation of this prayer is confirmed by the Apostolic See.

Given at the General Secretariat of the National Conference of Catholic Bishops, Washington, D.C., on August 15, 1995, the Solemnity of the Assumption of the Blessed Virgin Mary.

✝ William Cardinal Keeler
Archbishop of Baltimore
President
National Conference of Catholic Bishops

Dennis M. Schnurr
General Secretary

CONGREGATION FOR DIVINE WORSHIP
AND THE DISCIPLINE OF THE SACRAMENTS

Prot. N. 92/95/L

9 May 1995

Your Eminence,

This Congregation has received and examined the request of the National Conference of Catholic Bishops for the confirmation for the interim use of the ICEL translation of the *Eucharistic Prayers for Various Needs and Occasions.*

It has been decided that with this present letter permission is given to use this text only after the enclosed modifications have been made and may continue in use until such time as the new translation of the Roman Missal is presented for confirmation.

With every prayerful good wish, I remain,

Yours sincerely in Christ,

✝ Antonio M. Cardinal Javierre
Prefect

✝ Geraldo M. Agnelo
Archbishop Secretary

His Eminence William Cardinal Keeler
President
National Conference of Catholic Bishops
1312 Massachusetts Avenue, N.W.
Washington, D.C. 20005-4105 U.S.A.

CONGREGATION FOR DIVINE WORSHIP
AND THE DISCIPLINE OF THE SACRAMENTS

Prot. CD 511/91

DECREE

By its very nature the eucharistic prayer is, as it were, the summit of the entire celebration of the Mass. The purpose of this prayer, a prayer of thanksgiving and sanctification, is that the entire congregation joins itself to Christ in acknowledging the great things God has done and in offering the paschal sacrifice. The nature and purpose of the eucharistic prayer are always found in the various formularies in which this prayer is expressed.

Nevertheless, regarding the purpose of the eucharistic prayer there is one particular element to which attention must be given, namely, that of petition or intercession. For that reason the revised *Missale Romanum* provides various intercessory formulas for particular celebrations, primarily for the celebration of Ritual Masses. These formulas are to be inserted into each of the eucharistic prayers in conformity with the structure of each prayer.

For that same reason, after the *Missale Romanum* with its four eucharistic prayers had been issued for the universal Roman Rite, some conferences of bishops sought the Apostolic See's approval of new eucharistic prayers for use on the occasion of some commemoration or special event. Among those texts is the one that had been prepared for the occasion of the celebration of the Synod of the dioceses of Switzerland. Approval has been granted for such prayers in individual cases within the limits provided for by liturgical law.

Over the course of time, permission to use the text approved in 1974 for the Swiss Synod has been granted by the Holy See to various countries after a petition had been made by the conferences which had prepared a translation of the text into their own languages.

Since from the very beginning different editions of the text of this eucharistic prayer have been available in German, French, and Italian, it seems necessary to issue a Latin text of this prayer to serve as the *editio typica* for all languages.

To meet this need, the Congregation for Divine Worship and the Discipline of the Sacraments is now publishing a Latin version of the above-mentioned prayer and declares it to be the typical edition, so that vernacular versions prepared in the future may faithfully follow it.

Moreover, all vernacular versions already approved must in the future be made to agree with this Latin typical edition when new editions of the *Missale Romanum* are published in these languages after confirmation by the Holy See. Previous vernacular versions are then abrogated.

As its structure and text clearly show, from its origins this prayer was prepared in such a way that it could respond to various circumstances. Therefore the use of this text, on the part of all who have obtained or will obtain permission for it, will follow the norms established in this typical edition, so that the text of the prayer may be used in harmony with the formularies of the Masses for Various Needs and Occasions.

All things to the contrary notwithstanding.

From the Office of the Congregation for Divine Worship and the Discipline of the Sacraments, 6 August 1991, Feast of the Transfiguration of the Lord.

✠ Eduardo Cardinal Martinez
Prefect

✠ Lajos Kada
Titular Archbishop of Tibica
Secretary

INTRODUCTION

1   This eucharistic prayer with its proper prefaces and corresponding intercessions may be used with the formularies of the Masses for Various Needs and Occasions, which do not have their own proper preface.

2   The preface entitled "The Church on the Way to Unity" and its intercession may suitably be used, for example, with the formularies of the Masses "For the Universal Church," "For the Pope," "For the Bishop," "For the Election of a Pope or Bishop," "For a Council or Synod," "For Priests," "For the Priest Himself," "For the Ministers of the Church," and "For Pastoral or Spiritual Meetings."

3   The preface entitled "God Guides the Church on the Way of Salvation" and its intercession may suitably be used, for example, with the formularies of the Masses "For the Universal Church," "For Priestly Vocations," "For Religious," "For the Laity," "In Thanksgiving," "For the Family," "For Relatives and Friends," and "For Charity."

4   The preface entitled "Jesus, Way to the Father" and its intercession may suitably be used, for example, with the formularies of the Masses "For the Spread of the Gospel," "For Persecuted Christians," "For the Nation, (State,) or City," "For Those Who Serve in Public Office," "For the Assembly of National Leaders," "For the Progress of Peoples," and "Beginning of the Civil Year."

5   The preface entitled "Jesus, the Compassion of God" and its intercession may suitably be used, for example, with the formularies of the Masses "In Time of Famine or for Those who Suffer from Famine," "For Refugees and Exiles," "For those Unjustly Deprived of Liberty," "For Prisoners," "For the Sick," "For the Dying," "For Any Need," "For Our Oppressors," and "For a Happy Death."

6   At concelebrated Masses the prayer is said in the following way:

    1.   The preface and the words after the Sanctus from "You are truly blessed" to "breaks the bread" are said only by the presiding celebrant, with hands outstretched.

    2.   All the concelebrants say together the words from "Great and merciful Father" to "Lord, Jesus Christ," with hands outstretched toward the offerings.

3.   All the concelebrants say together the words from "On the eve of his passion and death" to "whose body and blood we share," in the following way:

—They say "On the eve of his passion and death" and "when supper was ended," with hands joined.

—If it seems appropriate, they may hold the right hand extended toward the bread and the cup during the words of the Lord in the institution narrative. After the eucharistic bread and the cup are shown to the people, they make a low bow when the presiding celebrant genuflects.

—During the anamnesis "And so, Father most holy" and the offering "Look with favor" and during the second epiclesis "Through the power," the concelebrating priests hold their hands outstretched.

4.   The intercessions "Renew by the light of the gospel" or "Strengthen in unity" or "Almighty Father" or "Lord, perfect your Church" may be assigned by the presiding celebrant to one or other of the concelebrating priests, who says them alone, with hands outstretched..

5.   The following parts of the eucharistic prayer may be sung: "On the eve of his passion and death," "When supper was ended," "And so, Father most holy," "Look with favor," and also the final doxology.

EUCHARISTIC PRAYER FOR MASSES FOR VARIOUS NEEDS AND OCCASIONS

I. The Church on the Way to Unity

The first form of the eucharistic prayer has as its theme ''The Church on the Way to Unity'' and may suitably be used, for example, with the formularies of the Masses ''For the Universal Church,'' ''For the Pope,'' ''For the Bishop,'' ''For the Election of a Pope or Bishop,'' ''For a Council or Synod,'' ''For Priests,'' ''For the Priest Himself,'' ''For the Ministers of the Church,'' and ''For Pastoral or Spiritual Meetings.''

The priest begins the eucharistic prayer. With hands extended, the priest sings or says:	**The Lord be with you.**
The people answer:	**And also with you.**
He lifts up his hands and continues:	**Lift up your hearts.**
The people answer:	**We lift them up to the Lord.**
With hands extended, he continues:	**Let us give thanks to the Lord our God.**
The people answer:	**It is right to give him thanks and praise.**

The priest continues the preface with hands extended.

It is truly right to give you thanks,
it is fitting that we sing of your glory,
Father of infinite goodness.

Through the gospel proclaimed by your Son
you have brought together in a single
   Church
people of every nation, culture, and tongue.
Into it you breathe the power of your Spirit,
that in every age
your children may be gathered as one.

Your Church bears steadfast witness to your
   love.
It nourishes our hope for the coming of your
   kingdom
and is a sure sign of the lasting covenant
which you promised us in Jesus Christ our
   Lord.

Therefore heaven and earth sing forth your
   praise
while we, with all the Church,
proclaim your glory without end:

At the end of the preface, he joins his hands and, together with the people, concludes it by singing or saying aloud:

Holy, holy, holy Lord, God of power and
   might,
heaven and earth are full of your glory.
   Hosanna in the highest.
Blessed is he who comes in the name of the
   Lord.
   Hosanna in the highest.

The prayer continues on page 16.

The priest begins the eucharistic prayer. With hands extended, the priest sings:

The Lord—— be with you.

The people answer:

And al - so with you.

He lifts up his hands and continues:

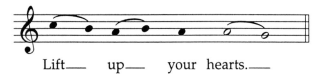

Lift—— up—— your hearts.——

The people answer:

We lift— them up to the Lord.——

With hands extended, he continues:

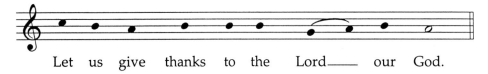

Let us give thanks to the Lord—— our God.

The people answer:

It is right to give him thanks—— and praise.——

The priest continues the preface with hands extended.

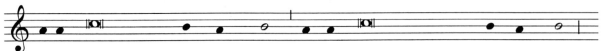

It is truly right to give you thanks, it is fitting that we sing of your glory,

At the end of the preface, he joins his hands and, together with the people, concludes it by singing:

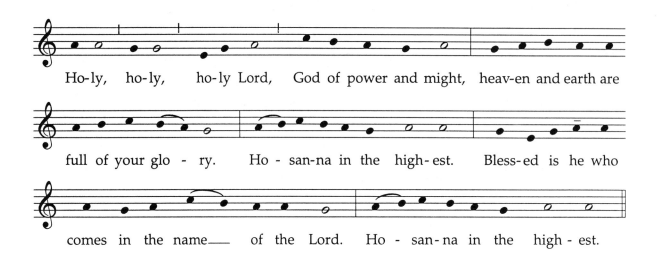

Ho-ly, ho-ly, ho-ly Lord, God of power and might, heav-en and earth are full of your glo - ry. Ho - san-na in the high-est. Bless-ed is he who comes in the name— of the Lord. Ho - san-na in the high - est.

The priest, with hands extended, says:

You are truly blessed, O God of holiness: you accompany us with love as we journey through life. Blessed too is your Son, Jesus Christ, who is present among us and whose love gathers us together. As once he did for his disciples, Christ now opens the scriptures for us and breaks the bread.

He joins his hands and, holding them outstretched over the offerings, says:

Great and merciful Father, we ask you to send down your Holy Spirit to hallow these gifts of bread and wine, that they may become for us

He joins his hands and, making the sign of the cross once over both bread and chalice, says:

the body ✠ and blood of our Lord, Jesus Christ.

He joins his hands.

The words of the Lord in the following formulas should be spoken clearly and distinctly, as their meaning demands.

**On the eve of his passion and death,
while at table with those he loved,**

He takes the bread and, raising it a little above the altar, continues:

**he took bread and gave you thanks;
he broke the bread,
gave it to his disciples, and said:**

He bows slightly.

**Take this, all of you, and eat it:
This is my body which will be given up
  for you.**

He shows the consecrated host to the people, places it on the paten, and genuflects in adoration.

Then he continues:

When supper was ended, he took the cup;

He takes the chalice and, raising it a little above the altar, continues:

**again he gave you thanks
and, handing the cup to his disciples, he
  said:**

He bows slightly.

**Take this, all of you, and drink from it:
This is the cup of my blood,
the blood of the new and everlasting
  covenant.
It will be shed for you and for all
so that sins may be forgiven.**

Do this in memory of me.

He shows the chalice to the people, places it on the corporal, and genuflects in adoration.

Then he sings:

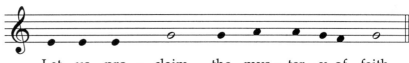

Let us pro - claim the mys - ter - y of faith.

People with celebrant and concelebrants:

A

Christ has died, Christ is ris - en, Christ will come a - gain.

B

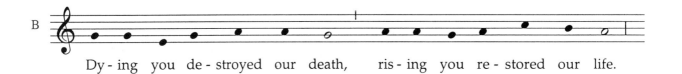

Dy - ing you de - stroyed our death, ris - ing you re - stored our life.

Lord___ Je - sus, come in glo - ry.

C

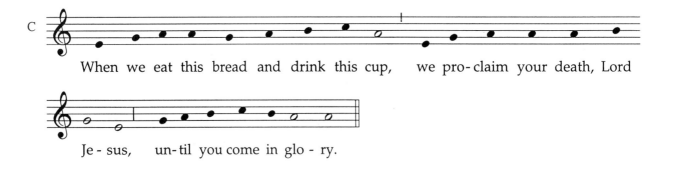

When we eat this bread and drink this cup, we pro - claim your death, Lord

Je - sus, un - til you come in glo - ry.

D

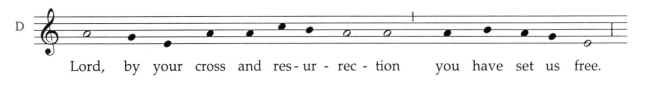

Lord, by your cross and res - ur - rec - tion you have set us free.

You are the Sav - ior of the world.

Then, with hands extended, the priest says:

And so, Father most holy,
we celebrate the memory of Christ, your Son,
whom you led through suffering and death on the cross
to the glory of the resurrection
and a place at your right hand.
Until Jesus, our Savior, comes again,
we proclaim the work of your love,
and we offer you the bread of life
and the cup of eternal blessing.

Look with favor on the offering of your Church
in which we show forth the paschal sacrifice of Christ
entrusted to us.
Through the power of your Spirit of love
include us now and for ever
among the members of your Son,
whose body and blood we share.

With hands extended, the priest continues:

Renew by the light of the gospel
the Church of N. [diocese/place].
Strengthen the bonds of unity between the faithful and their pastors,
that together with N. our pope, N. our bishop,
and the whole college of bishops,
your people may stand forth
in a world torn by strife and discord
as a sign of oneness and peace.

Be mindful of our brothers and sisters [N. and N.],
who have fallen asleep in the peace of Christ,
and all the dead whose faith only you can know.
Lead them to the fullness of the resurrection
and gladden them with the light of your face.

When our pilgrimage on earth is complete,
welcome us into your heavenly home,
where we shall dwell with you for ever.
There, with Mary, the Virgin Mother of God,
with the apostles, the martyrs,
[Saint N.,] and all the saints,
we shall praise you and give you glory

He joins his hands.

through Jesus Christ, your Son.

He takes the chalice and paten with the host and, lifting them up, sings:

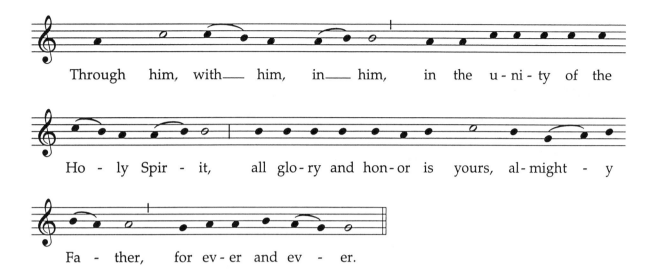

Through him, with— him, in— him, in the u-ni-ty of the

Ho-ly Spir-it, all glo-ry and hon-or is yours, al-might-y

Fa-ther, for ev-er and ev-er.

The people respond: A-men.——

Or, in place of the single *Amen*, the following may be sung:

A - men.——   A - men.——   A - men.

EUCHARISTIC PRAYER FOR MASSES FOR VARIOUS NEEDS AND OCCASIONS

II. God Guides the Church on the Way of Salvation

The second form of the eucharistic prayer has as its theme "God Guides the Church on the Way of Salvation" and may suitably be used, for example, with the formularies of the Masses "For the Universal Church," "For Priestly Vocations," "For Religious," "For the Laity," "In Thanksgiving," "For the Family," "For Relatives and Friends," and "For Charity."

The priest begins the eucharistic prayer. With hands extended, the priest sings or says:	**The Lord be with you.**
The people answer:	**And also with you.**
He lifts up his hands and continues:	**Lift up your hearts.**
The people answer:	**We lift them up to the Lord.**
With hands extended, he continues:	**Let us give thanks to the Lord our God.**
The people answer:	**It is right to give him thanks and praise.**

The priest continues the preface with hands extended.

**It is truly right and just,
our duty and our salvation
always and everywhere to give you thanks,
Lord, holy Father,
creator of the world and source of all life.**

**You never abandon the creatures formed by
your wisdom,
but remain with us and work for our good
even now.
With mighty hand and outstretched arm
you led your people, Israel, through the
desert.
By the power of the Holy Spirit
you guide your pilgrim Church today
as it journeys along the paths of time
to the eternal joy of your kingdom,
through Christ our Lord.**

**Now, with all the angels and saints
we praise your glory without end:**

At the end of the preface, he joins his hands and, together with the people, concludes it by singing or saying aloud:

**Holy, holy, holy Lord, God of power and
might,
heaven and earth are full of your glory.
Hosanna in the highest.
Blessed is he who comes in the name of the
Lord.
Hosanna in the highest.**

The prayer continues on page 26.

The priest begins the eucharistic prayer. With hands extended, the priest sings:

The Lord — be with you.

The people answer:

And al - so with you.

He lifts up his hands and continues:

Lift — up — your hearts. —

The people answer:

We lift — them up to the Lord. —

With hands extended, he continues:

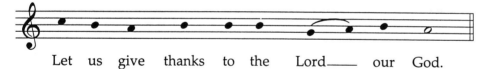

Let us give thanks to the Lord — our God.

The people answer:

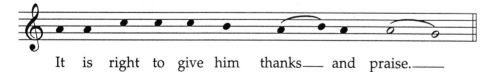

It is right to give him thanks — and praise. —

The priest continues the preface with hands extended.

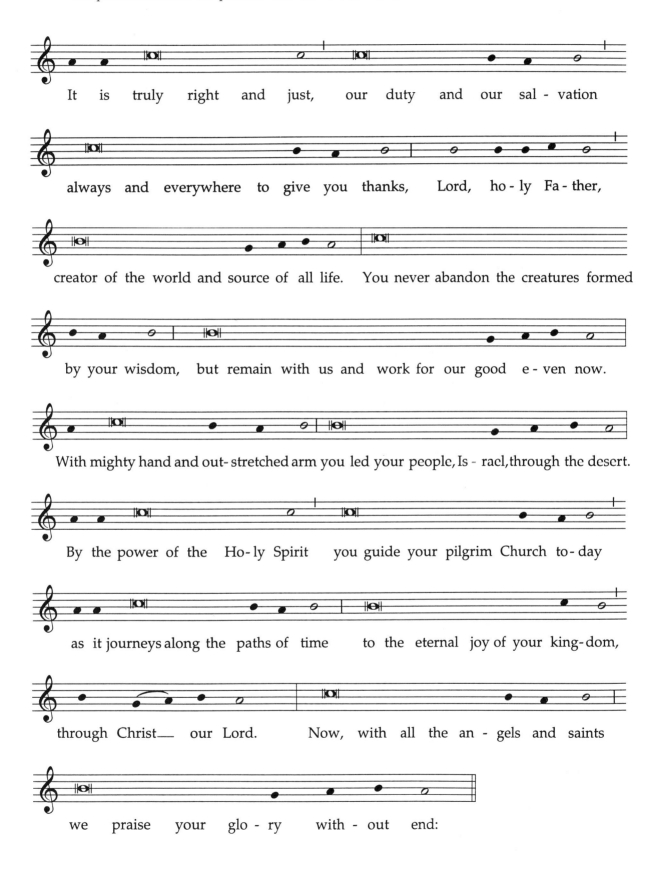

It is truly right and just, our duty and our sal - vation

always and everywhere to give you thanks, Lord, ho - ly Fa - ther,

creator of the world and source of all life. You never abandon the creatures formed

by your wisdom, but remain with us and work for our good e - ven now.

With mighty hand and out-stretched arm you led your people, Is - rael, through the desert.

By the power of the Ho-ly Spirit you guide your pilgrim Church to-day

as it journeys along the paths of time to the eternal joy of your king-dom,

through Christ— our Lord. Now, with all the an - gels and saints

we praise your glo - ry with - out end:

At the end of the preface, he joins his hands and, together with the people, concludes it by singing:

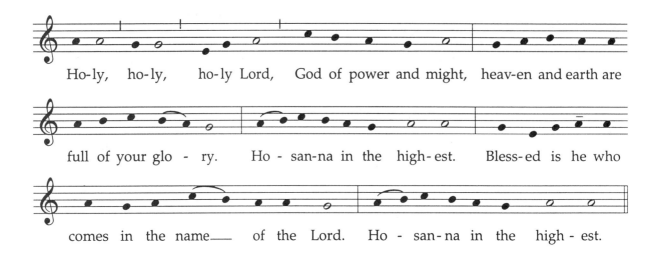

Ho-ly, ho-ly, ho-ly Lord, God of power and might, heav-en and earth are full of your glo-ry. Ho-san-na in the high-est. Bless-ed is he who comes in the name—— of the Lord. Ho-san-na in the high-est.

The priest, with hands extended, says:

You are truly blessed, O God of holiness: you accompany us with love as we journey through life. Blessed too is your Son, Jesus Christ, who is present among us and whose love gathers us together. As once he did for his disciples, Christ now opens the scriptures for us and breaks the bread.

He joins his hands and, holding them outstretched over the offerings, says:

Great and merciful Father, we ask you to send down your Holy Spirit to hallow these gifts of bread and wine, that they may become for us

He joins his hands and, making the sign of the cross once over both bread and chalice, says:

the body ✠ and blood of our Lord, Jesus Christ.

He joins his hands.

The words of the Lord in the following formulas should be spoken clearly and distinctly, as their meaning demands.

On the eve of his passion and death, while at table with those he loved,

He takes the bread and, raising it a little above the altar, continues:

**he took bread and gave you thanks;
he broke the bread,
gave it to his disciples, and said:**

He bows slightly.

**Take this, all of you, and eat it:
This is my body which will be given up
   for you.**

He shows the consecrated host to the people, places it on the paten, and genuflects in adoration.

Then he continues:

When supper was ended, he took the cup;

He takes the chalice and, raising it a little above the altar, continues:

**again he gave you thanks
and, handing the cup to his disciples, he
   said:**

He bows slightly.

**Take this, all of you, and drink from it:
This is the cup of my blood,
the blood of the new and everlasting
   covenant.
It will be shed for you and for all
so that sins may be forgiven.**

Do this in memory of me.

He shows the chalice to the people, places it on the corporal, and genuflects in adoration.

Then he sings: Let us pro-claim the mys-ter-y of faith.

People with celebrant and concelebrants:

A

Christ has died, Christ is ris-en, Christ will come a-gain.

B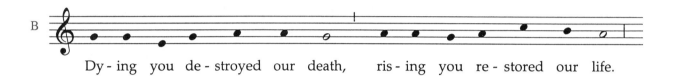

Dy-ing you de-stroyed our death, ris-ing you re-stored our life.

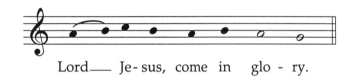

Lord___ Je-sus, come in glo-ry.

C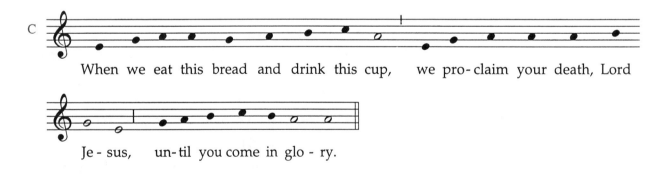

When we eat this bread and drink this cup, we pro-claim your death, Lord Je-sus, un-til you come in glo-ry.

D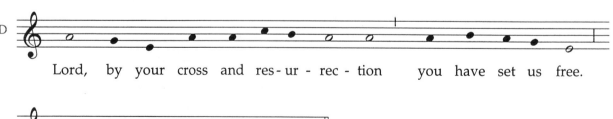

Lord, by your cross and res-ur-rec-tion you have set us free.

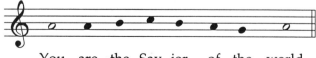

You are the Sav-ior of the world.

Then, with hands extended, the
priest says:

And so, Father most holy,
we celebrate the memory of Christ, your
    Son,
whom you led through suffering and death
    on the cross
to the glory of the resurrection
and a place at your right hand.
Until Jesus, our Savior, comes again,
we proclaim the work of your love,
and we offer you the bread of life
and the cup of eternal blessing.

Look with favor on the offering of your
    Church
in which we show forth the paschal sacri-
    fice of Christ
entrusted to us.
Through the power of your Spirit of love
include us now and for ever
among the members of your Son,
whose body and blood we share.

With hands extended, the priest
continues:

Strengthen in unity
those you have called to this table.
Together with N. our pope, N. our bishop,
with all bishops, priests, and deacons,
and all your holy people,
may we follow your paths in faith and hope
and radiate our joy and trust to all the world.

Be mindful of our brothers and sisters [N. and N.],
who have fallen asleep in the peace of Christ,
and all the dead whose faith only you can know.
Lead them to the fullness of the resurrection
and gladden them with the light of your face.

When our pilgrimage on earth is complete,
welcome us into your heavenly home,
where we shall dwell with you for ever.
There, with Mary, the Virgin Mother of God,
with the apostles, the martyrs,
[Saint N.,] and all the saints,
we shall praise you and give you glory

He joins his hands.

through Jesus Christ, your Son.

He takes the chalice and paten with the host and, lifting them up, sings:

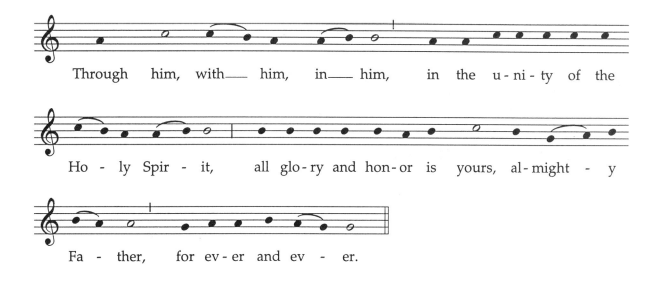

Through him, with— him, in— him, in the u-ni-ty of the Ho - ly Spir - it, all glo-ry and hon-or is yours, al-might - y Fa - ther, for ev-er and ev - er.

The people respond: A - men.———

Or, in place of the single *Amen*, the following may be sung:

A - men.———   A - men.———   A - men.

EUCHARISTIC PRAYER FOR MASSES FOR VARIOUS NEEDS AND OCCASIONS

III. Jesus, Way to the Father

The third form of the eucharistic prayer has as its theme "Jesus, Way to the Father" and may suitably be used, for example, with the formularies of the Masses "For the Spread of the Gospel," "For Persecuted Christians," "For the Nation, (State,) or City," "For Those Who Serve in Public Office," "For the Assembly of National Leaders," "For the Progress of Peoples," and "Beginning of the Civil Year."

The priest begins the eucharistic prayer. With hands extended, the priest sings or says:

The Lord be with you.

The people answer:

And also with you.

He lifts up his hands and continues:

Lift up your hearts.

The people answer:

We lift them up to the Lord.

With hands extended, he continues:

Let us give thanks to the Lord our God.

The people answer:

It is right to give him thanks and praise.

The priest continues the preface with hands extended.

It is truly right and just,
our duty and our salvation
always and everywhere to give you thanks,
Father of holiness, Lord of heaven and earth,
through our Lord Jesus Christ.

Through your eternal Word you created all
**   things**
and govern their course with infinite
**   wisdom.**
In the Word made flesh
you have given us a mediator
who has spoken your words to us
and called us to follow him.
He is the way that leads to you,
the truth that sets us free,
the life that makes our joy complete.
Through your Son
you gather into one family
men and women created for the glory of your
**   name,**
redeemed by the blood of the cross,
and sealed with the Holy Spirit.

And so we praise your mighty deeds
and join with the hosts of angels,
as they proclaim your glory without end:

At the end of the preface, he joins his hands and, together with the people, concludes it by singing or saying aloud:

Holy, holy, holy Lord, God of power and
**   might,**
heaven and earth are full of your glory.
** Hosanna in the highest.**
Blessed is he who comes in the name of the
**   Lord.**
** Hosanna in the highest.**

The prayer continues on page 36.

The priest begins the eucharistic prayer. With hands extended, the priest sings:

The Lord— be with you.

The people answer:

And al - so with you.

He lifts up his hands and continues:

Lift— up— your hearts.—

The people answer:

We lift— them up to the Lord.—

With hands extended, he continues:

Let us give thanks to the Lord— our God.

The people answer:

It is right to give him thanks— and praise.—

The priest continues the preface with hands extended.

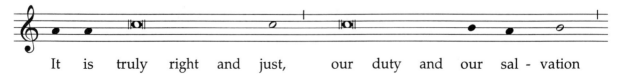

It is truly right and just, our duty and our sal - vation

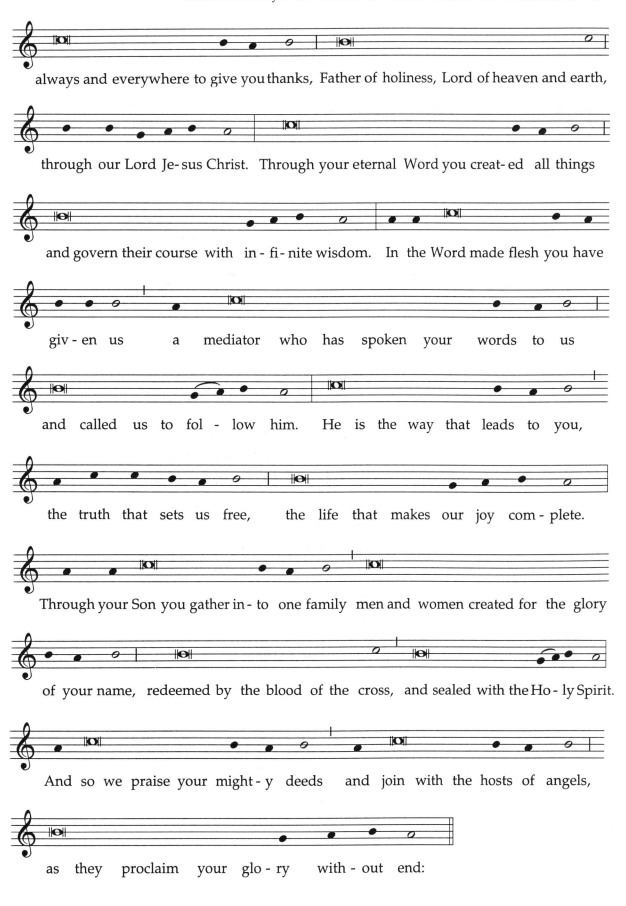

always and everywhere to give you thanks, Father of holiness, Lord of heaven and earth,

through our Lord Je-sus Christ.   Through your eternal Word you creat-ed all things

and govern their course with in - fi - nite wisdom.   In the Word made flesh you have

giv - en us   a   mediator   who has   spoken your   words   to   us

and   called   us   to fol - low him.   He is the way that leads to you,

the truth that sets us free,   the life that makes our joy com - plete.

Through your Son you gather in - to one family men and women created for the glory

of your name, redeemed by the blood of the cross, and sealed with the Ho - ly Spirit.

And so we praise your might - y deeds   and join with the hosts of angels,

as   they   proclaim   your   glo - ry   with - out   end:

At the end of the preface, he joins his hands and, together with the people, concludes it by singing:

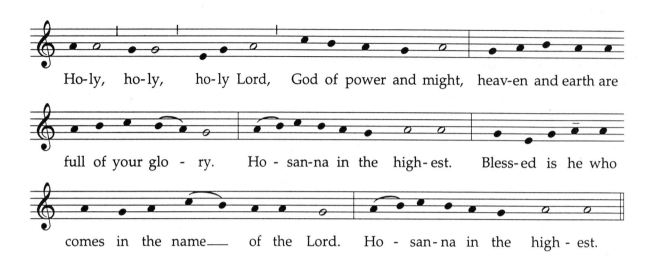

Ho-ly, ho-ly, ho-ly Lord, God of power and might, heav-en and earth are full of your glo - ry. Ho - san-na in the high- est. Bless-ed is he who comes in the name___ of the Lord. Ho - san-na in the high - est.

The priest, with hands extended, says:

You are truly blessed, O God of holiness:
you accompany us with love
as we journey through life.
Blessed too is your Son, Jesus Christ,
who is present among us
and whose love gathers us together.
As once he did for his disciples,
Christ now opens the scriptures for us
and breaks the bread.

He joins his hands and, holding them outstretched over the offerings, says:

Great and merciful Father,
we ask you to send down your Holy Spirit
to hallow these gifts of bread and wine,
that they may become for us

He joins his hands and, making the sign of the cross once over both bread and chalice, says:

the body ✚ and blood of our Lord, Jesus
Christ.

He joins his hands.

The words of the Lord in the following formulas should be spoken clearly and distinctly, as their meaning demands.

On the eve of his passion and death, while at table with those he loved,

He takes the bread and, raising it a little above the altar, continues:

he took bread and gave you thanks; he broke the bread, gave it to his disciples, and said:

He bows slightly.

Take this, all of you, and eat it: This is my body which will be given up for you.

He shows the consecrated host to the people, places it on the paten, and genuflects in adoration.

Then he continues:

When supper was ended, he took the cup;

He takes the chalice and, raising it a little above the altar, continues:

again he gave you thanks and, handing the cup to his disciples, he said:

He bows slightly.

Take this, all of you, and drink from it: This is the cup of my blood, the blood of the new and everlasting covenant. It will be shed for you and for all so that sins may be forgiven.

Do this in memory of me.

He shows the chalice to the people, places it on the corporal, and genuflects in adoration.

Then he sings:

Let us pro - claim   the mys - ter - y of faith.

People with celebrant and concelebrants:

A

Christ   has   died,   Christ   is   ris - en,   Christ   will   come   a - gain.

B
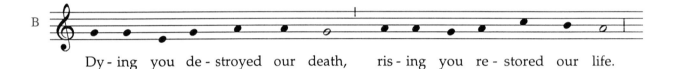
Dy - ing   you   de - stroyed   our   death,   ris - ing   you   re - stored   our   life.

Lord___ Je - sus, come in   glo - ry.

C
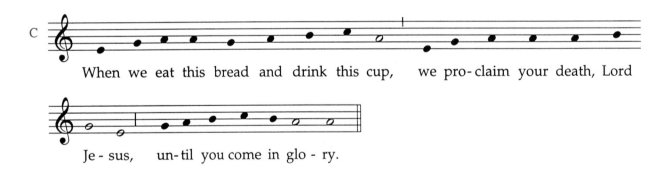
When we eat this bread and drink this cup,   we pro - claim your death, Lord

Je - sus,   un - til you come in glo - ry.

D
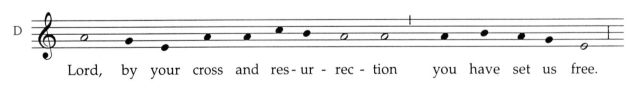
Lord,   by your cross and res - ur - rec - tion   you have set us free.

You   are   the Sav - ior   of   the world.

Then, with hands extended, the
priest says:

And so, Father most holy,
we celebrate the memory of Christ, your
    Son,
whom you led through suffering and death
    on the cross
to the glory of the resurrection
and a place at your right hand.
Until Jesus, our Savior, comes again,
we proclaim the work of your love,
and we offer you the bread of life
and the cup of eternal blessing.

Look with favor on the offering of your
    Church
in which we show forth the paschal sacri-
    fice of Christ
entrusted to us.
Through the power of your Spirit of love
include us now and for ever
among the members of your Son,
whose body and blood we share.

With hands extended, the priest
continues:

Almighty Father,
by our sharing in this mystery
enliven us with your Spirit
and conform us to the image of your Son.
Strengthen the bonds of our communion
with N. our pope, N. our bishop,
with all bishops, priests, and deacons,
and all your holy people.

Keep your Church alert in faith to the signs
of the times
and eager to accept the challenge of the
gospel.
Open our hearts to the needs of all humanity,
so that sharing their grief and anguish,
their joy and hope,
we may faithfully bring them the good news
of salvation
and advance together on the way to your
kingdom.

Be mindful of our brothers and sisters [N.
and N.],
who have fallen asleep in the peace of
Christ,
and all the dead whose faith only you can
know.
Lead them to the fullness of the resurrection
and gladden them with the light of your
face.

When our pilgrimage on earth is complete,
welcome us into your heavenly home,
where we shall dwell with you for ever.
There, with Mary, the Virgin Mother of
God,
with the apostles, the martyrs,
[Saint N.,] and all the saints,
we shall praise you and give you glory

He joins his hands.

through Jesus Christ, your Son.

He takes the chalice and paten with the host and, lifting them up, sings:

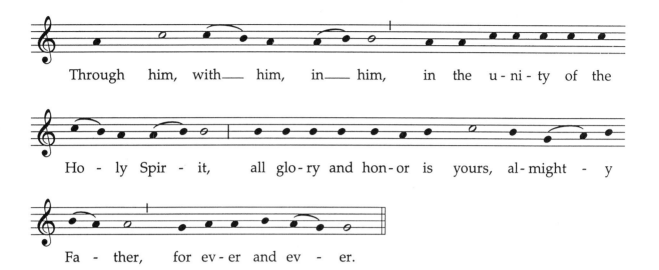

Through him, with— him, in— him, in the u-ni-ty of the

Ho - ly Spir - it, all glo-ry and hon-or is yours, al-might - y

Fa - ther, for ev-er and ev - er.

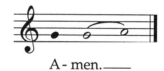

The people respond:

A- men.——

Or, in place of the single *Amen*, the following may be sung:

A - men.—— A - men.—— A - men.

EUCHARISTIC PRAYER FOR MASSES
FOR VARIOUS NEEDS AND OCCASIONS
IV. Jesus, the Compassion of God

The fourth form of the eucharistic prayer has as its theme "Jesus, the Compassion of God" and may suitably be used, for example, with the formularies of the Masses "In Time of Famine or for Those who Suffer from Famine," "For Refugees and Exiles," "For those Unjustly Deprived of Liberty," "For Prisoners," "For the Sick," "For the Dying," "For Any Need," "For Our Oppressors," and "For a Happy Death."

The priest begins the eucharistic prayer. With hands extended, the priest sings or says:

The Lord be with you.

The people answer:

And also with you.

He lifts up his hands and continues:

Lift up your hearts.

The people answer:

We lift them up to the Lord.

With hands extended, he continues:

Let us give thanks to the Lord our God.

The people answer:

It is right to give him thanks and praise.

The priest continues the preface with hands extended.

**It is truly right to give you thanks,
it is fitting that we offer you praise,
Father of mercy, faithful God.**

**You sent Jesus Christ your Son among us
as redeemer and Lord.
He was moved with compassion
for the poor and the powerless,
for the sick and the sinner;
he made himself neighbor to the oppressed.
By his words and actions
he proclaimed to the world
that you care for us
as a father cares for his children.**

**And so, with all the angels and saints
we sing the joyful hymn of your praise:**

At the end of the preface, he joins his hands and, together with the people, concludes it by singing or saying aloud:

**Holy, holy, holy Lord, God of power and
     might,
heaven and earth are full of your glory.
   Hosanna in the highest.
Blessed is he who comes in the name of the
     Lord.
   Hosanna in the highest.**

The prayer continues on page 46.

The priest begins the eucharistic prayer. With hands extended, the priest sings:

The Lord—— be with you.

The people answer:

And al - so with you.

He lifts up his hands and continues:

Lift—— up—— your hearts.——

The people answer:

We lift— them up to the Lord.——

With hands extended, he continues:

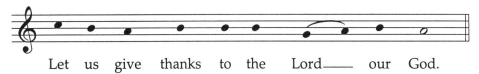

Let us give thanks to the Lord—— our God.

The people answer:

It is right to give him thanks—— and praise.——

The priest continues the preface with hands extended.

It is truly right to give you thanks, it is fitting that we of-fer you praise, Father of mercy, faith - ful God. You sent Jesus Christ your Son a - mong us as re deem-er and Lord. He was moved with compassion for the poor and the powerless, for the sick and the sinner; he made himself neighbor to the op - pressed. By his words and actions he pro-claimed to the world that you care for us as a father cares for his children. And so, with all the an-gels and saints we sing the joyful hymn of your praise:

At the end of the preface, he joins his hands and, together with the people, concludes it by singing:

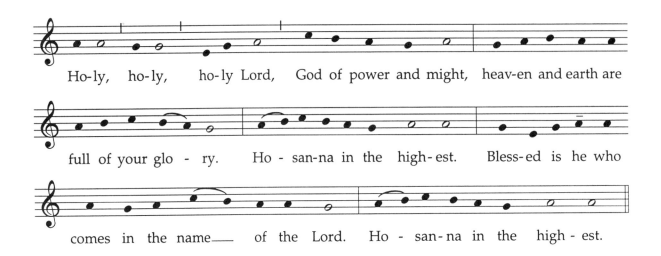

Ho-ly, ho-ly, ho-ly Lord, God of power and might, heav-en and earth are full of your glo - ry. Ho - san-na in the high-est. Bless-ed is he who comes in the name—— of the Lord. Ho - san-na in the high - est.

The priest, with hands extended, says:

**You are truly blessed, O God of holiness:
you accompany us with love
as we journey through life.
Blessed too is your Son, Jesus Christ,
who is present among us
and whose love gathers us together.
As once he did for his disciples,
Christ now opens the scriptures for us
and breaks the bread.**

He joins his hands and, holding them outstretched over the offerings, says:

**Great and merciful Father,
we ask you to send down your Holy Spirit
to hallow these gifts of bread and wine,
that they may become for us**

He joins his hands and, making the sign of the cross once over both bread and chalice, says:

the body ✝ and blood of our Lord, Jesus Christ.

He joins his hands.

The words of the Lord in the following formulas should be spoken clearly and distinctly, as their meaning demands.

On the eve of his passion and death, while at table with those he loved,

He takes the bread and, raising it a little above the altar, continues:

he took bread and gave you thanks; he broke the bread, gave it to his disciples, and said:

He bows slightly.

Take this, all of you, and eat it: This is my body which will be given up for you.

He shows the consecrated host to the people, places it on the paten, and genuflects in adoration.

Then he continues:

When supper was ended, he took the cup;

He takes the chalice and, raising it a little above the altar, continues:

again he gave you thanks and, handing the cup to his disciples, he said:

He bows slightly.

Take this, all of you, and drink from it: This is the cup of my blood, the blood of the new and everlasting covenant. It will be shed for you and for all so that sins may be forgiven.

Do this in memory of me.

He shows the chalice to the people, places it on the corporal, and genuflects in adoration.

Then he sings: Let us pro - claim the mys - ter - y of faith.

People with celebrant and concelebrants:

A

Christ has died, Christ is ris - en, Christ will come a - gain.

B
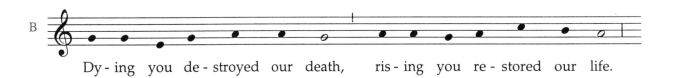

Dy - ing you de - stroyed our death, ris - ing you re - stored our life.

Lord— Je - sus, come in glo - ry.

C
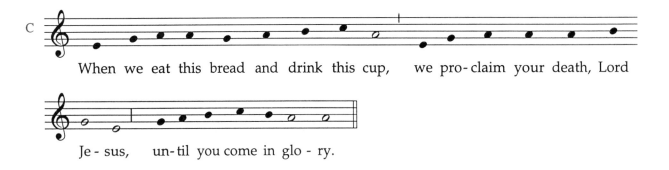

When we eat this bread and drink this cup, we pro - claim your death, Lord

Je - sus, un - til you come in glo - ry.

D
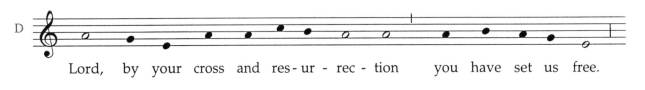

Lord, by your cross and res - ur - rec - tion you have set us free.

You are the Sav - ior of the world.

Then, with hands extended, the priest says:

And so, Father most holy,
we celebrate the memory of Christ, your
Son,
whom you led through suffering and death
on the cross
to the glory of the resurrection
and a place at your right hand.
Until Jesus, our Savior, comes again,
we proclaim the work of your love,
and we offer you the bread of life
and the cup of eternal blessing.

Look with favor on the offering of your
Church
in which we show forth the paschal sacri-
fice of Christ
entrusted to us.
Through the power of your Spirit of love
include us now and for ever
among the members of your Son,
whose body and blood we share.

With hands extended, the priest continues:

Lord,
perfect your Church in faith and love
together with N. our pope, N. our bishop,
with all bishops, priests, and deacons,
and all those your Son has gained for you.

Open our eyes to the needs of all;
inspire us with words and deeds
to comfort those who labor
and are burdened;
keep our service of others
faithful to the example and command of
Christ.

Let your Church be a living witness
to truth and freedom, to justice and peace,
that all people may be lifted up
by the hope of a world made new.

Be mindful of our brothers and sisters [N.
    and N.],
who have fallen asleep in the peace of
    Christ,
and all the dead whose faith only you can
    know.
Lead them to the fullness of the resurrection
and gladden them with the light of your
    face.

When our pilgrimage on earth is complete,
welcome us into your heavenly home,
where we shall dwell with you for ever.
There, with Mary, the Virgin Mother of
    God,
with the apostles, the martyrs,
[Saint N.,] and all the saints,
we shall praise you and give you glory

He joins his hands.   **through Jesus Christ, your Son.**

He takes the chalice and paten with the host and, lifting them up, sings:

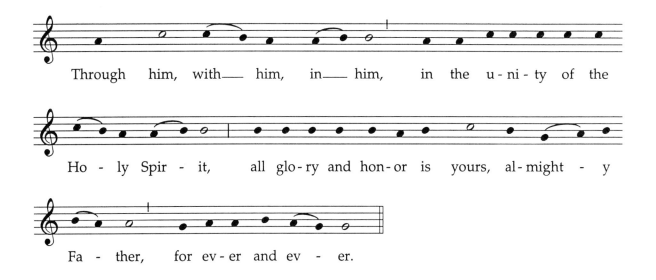

Through him, with— him, in— him, in the u - ni - ty of the

Ho - ly Spir - it, all glo-ry and hon-or is yours, al-might - y

Fa - ther, for ev - er and ev - er.

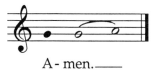

The people respond: A - men.——

Or, in place of the single *Amen*, the following may be sung:

A - men.——   A - men.——   A   -   men.

EUCHARISTIC PRAYER FOR MASSES
FOR VARIOUS NEEDS AND OCCASIONS

The priest leads the assembly in the eucharistic prayer. The people take part reverently and attentively and make the acclamations.

The priest begins the eucharistic prayer. With hands extended, the priest sings:

The Lord___ be with you.

The people answer:

And al - so with you.

He lifts up his hands and continues:

Lift___ up___ your hearts.___

The people answer:

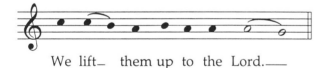

We lift_ them up to the Lord.___

With hands extended, he continues:

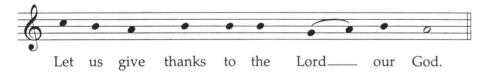

Let us give thanks to the Lord___ our God.

The people answer:

It is right to give him thanks___ and praise.___

The priest continues the preface with hands extended.

I. THE CHURCH ON THE WAY TO UNITY

It is truly right to give you thanks, it is fitting that we sing of your glory,

Father of in-fi-nite goodness. Through the gospel proclaimed by your Son

you have brought together in a sin-gle Church people of every nation,

cul-ture, and tongue. Into it you breathe the power of your Spirit,

that in every age your children may be gath-ered as one.

Your Church bears steadfast witness to your love.

It nourishes our hope for the coming of your kingdom

and is a sure sign of the lasting cov-enant which you promised us in Jesus

Christ— our Lord. Therefore heaven and earth sing forth your praise

while we, with all the Church, proclaim your glo-ry with-out end:

The prayer continues with the Sanctus on page 58.

II. GOD GUIDES THE CHURCH

It is truly right and just, our duty and our sal - vation

always and everywhere to give you thanks, Lord, ho - ly Fa - ther,

creator of the world and source of all life.   You never abandon the creatures formed

by your wisdom,   but remain with us and work for our good e - ven now.

With mighty hand and out- stretched arm you led your people, Is - rael, through the desert.

By the power of the Ho - ly Spirit   you guide your pilgrim Church to - day

as it journeys along the paths of time   to the eternal joy of your king - dom,

through Christ— our Lord.   Now, with all the an - gels and saints

we praise your glo - ry with - out end:

The prayer continues with the Sanctus on page 58.

III. JESUS, WAY TO THE FATHER

It is truly right and just, our duty and our sal - vation

always and everywhere to give you thanks, Father of holiness, Lord of heaven and earth,

through our Lord Je-sus Christ. Through your eternal Word you creat-ed all things

and govern their course with in - fi - nite wisdom. In the Word made flesh you have

giv - en us a mediator who has spoken your words to us

and called us to fol - low him. He is the way that leads to you,

the truth that sets us free, the life that makes our joy com - plete.

Through your Son you gather in - to one family men and women created for the glory

of your name, redeemed by the blood of the cross, and sealed with the Ho - ly Spirit.

And so we praise your might - y deeds and join with the hosts of angels,

as they proclaim your glo - ry with - out end:

The prayer continues with the Sanctus on page 58.

IV. JESUS, THE COMPASSION OF GOD

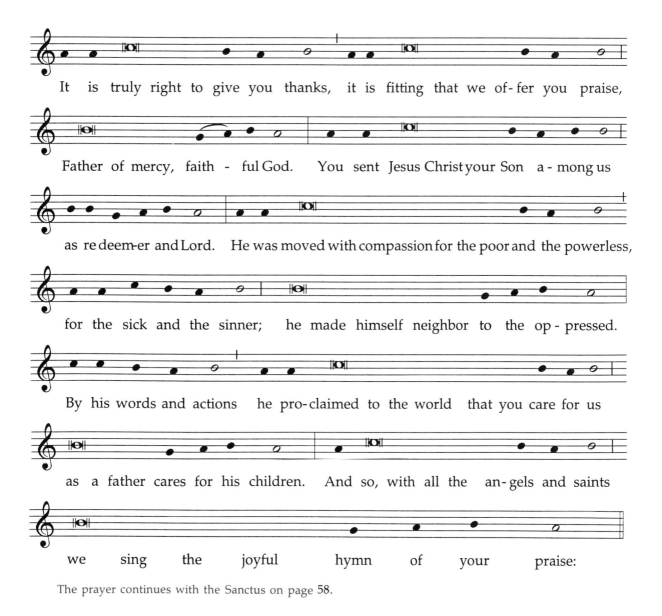

It is truly right to give you thanks, it is fitting that we of-fer you praise,

Father of mercy, faith - ful God.   You sent Jesus Christ your Son a - mong us

as re deem-er and Lord.   He was moved with compassion for the poor and the powerless,

for the sick and the sinner;   he made himself neighbor to the op - pressed.

By his words and actions   he pro-claimed to the world   that you care for us

as a father cares for his children.   And so, with all the   an- gels and saints

we sing the joyful hymn of your praise:

The prayer continues with the Sanctus on page 58.

At the end of the preface, he joins his hands and, together with the people, concludes it by singing:

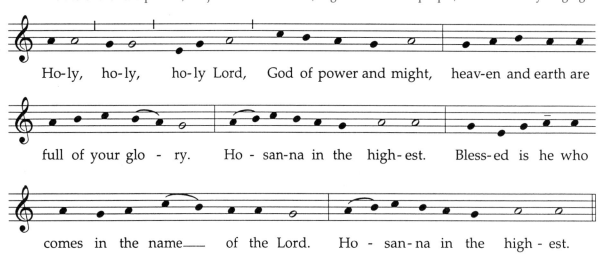

Ho-ly, ho-ly, ho-ly Lord, God of power and might, heav-en and earth are full of your glo - ry. Ho - san-na in the high-est. Bless-ed is he who comes in the name___ of the Lord. Ho - san-na in the high - est.

The priest, with hands extended, sings (the words in brackets may be omitted):

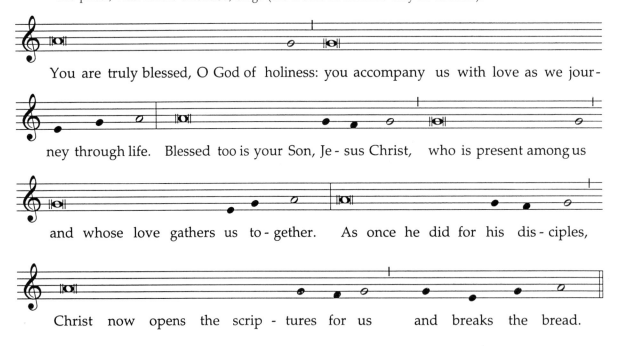

You are truly blessed, O God of holiness: you accompany us with love as we jour-ney through life. Blessed too is your Son, Je - sus Christ, who is present among us and whose love gathers us to - gether. As once he did for his dis - ciples, Christ now opens the scrip - tures for us and breaks the bread.

The cantor sings the following acclamation, and the people repeat it:

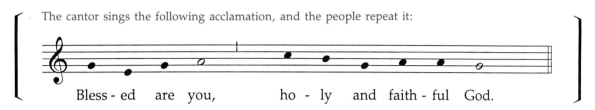

Bless - ed are you, ho - ly and faith - ful God.

He joins his hands and, holding them outstretched over the offerings, sings:

Great and merciful Father, we ask you to send down your Ho - ly Spirit

to hallow these gifts of bread and wine, that they may be - come for us the

He joins his hands, making the sign of the cross once over both bread and chalice, sings:

body ✠ and blood of our Lord, Je - sus Christ.

The people take up the acclamation:

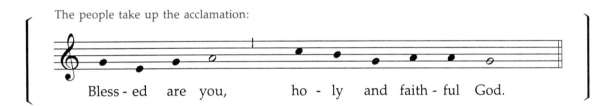

Bless - ed are you, ho - ly and faith - ful God.

The words of the Lord in the following formulas should be spoken clearly and distinctly, as their meaning demands.

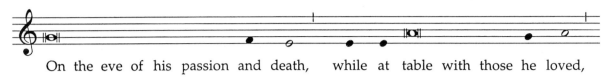

On the eve of his passion and death, while at table with those he loved,

He takes the bread and, raising it a little above the altar, continues:

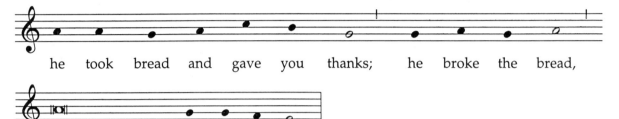

he took bread and gave you thanks; he broke the bread,

gave it to his dis - ci - ples, and said:

He bows slightly.

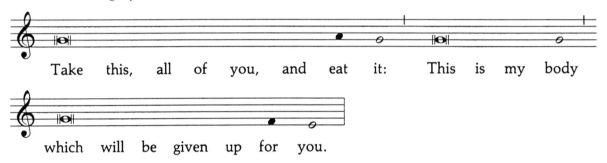

Take this, all of you, and eat it: This is my body

which will be given up for you.

He shows the consecrated host to the people, replaces it on the plate, and genuflects in adoration.

Then he continues:

He takes the chalice and, raising it a little above the altar, continues:

When supper was ended, he took the cup; a - gain he gave you thanks

and, handing the cup to his dis - ci - ples, he said:

He bows slightly.

Take this, all of you, and drink from it:

This is the cup of my blood,

the blood of the new and everlast - ing covenant.

It will be shed for you and for all, so that sins may be for-

giv - en. Do this in memory of me.

He shows the chalice to the people, replaces it on the corporal, and genuflects in adoration.

Then he sings:

Let us pro-claim the mys-ter-y of faith.

People with celebrant and concelebrants:

A

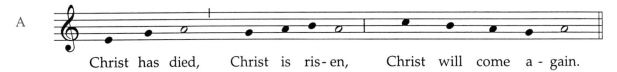

Christ has died, Christ is ris-en, Christ will come a-gain.

B

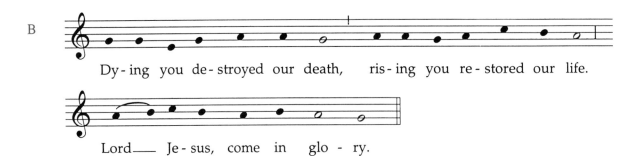

Dy-ing you de-stroyed our death, ris-ing you re-stored our life.

Lord—— Je-sus, come in glo-ry.

C

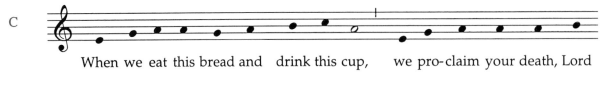

When we eat this bread and drink this cup, we pro-claim your death, Lord

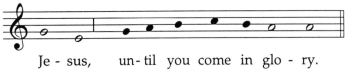

Je-sus, un-til you come in glo-ry.

D

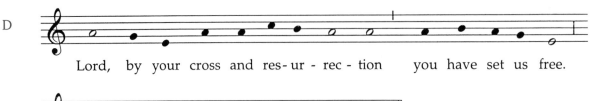

Lord, by your cross and res-ur-rec-tion you have set us free.

You are the Sav-ior of the world.

Then, with hands extended, the priest sings:

And so, Father most holy,   we celebrate the memory of Christ, your Son,

whom   you   led   through   suffering   and   death   on   the   cross

to the glory of the res - ur - rection   and   a   place - at   your   right   hand.

Until Jesus, our Savior, comes a - gain,   we   proclaim   the work of your love,

and we offer you the bread of life and the cup of e - ter - nal   bless - ing.

Look with favor on the offering of your Church in which we show forth the paschal

sacrifice of Christ entrusted to us.   Through the power of your Spir - it of love

in - clude us now and for ever   among the mem - bers of your Son,

whose body and blood we share.

The cantor sings the following acclamation and the people repeat it:

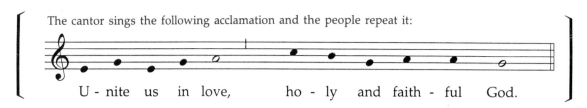

U - nite us in love, ho - ly and faith - ful God.

Then, with hands extended, the priest sings one of the following intercessions corresponding to the preface that was chosen at the beginning of the prayer.

I. THE CHURCH ON THE WAY TO UNITY

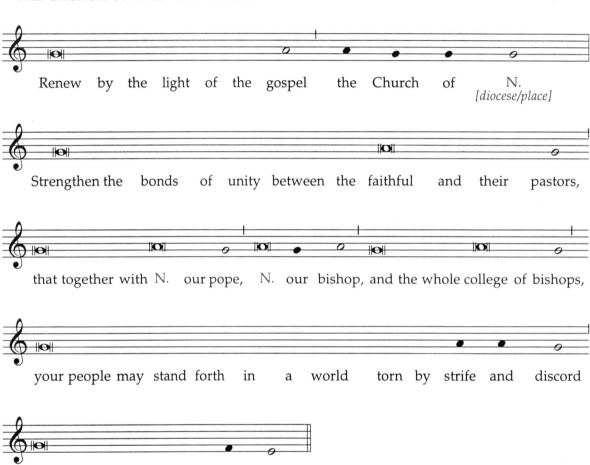

Renew by the light of the gospel the Church of N. *[diocese/place]*

Strengthen the bonds of unity between the faithful and their pastors,

that together with N. our pope, N. our bishop, and the whole college of bishops,

your people may stand forth in a world torn by strife and discord

as a sign of oneness and peace.

The people take up the acclamation:

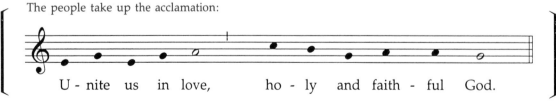

U - nite us in love, ho - ly and faith - ful God.

With hands extended, the priest continues the prayer on page 70.

II. GOD GUIDES THE CHURCH

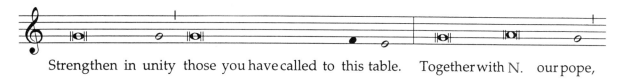

Strengthen in unity those you have called to this table.   Together with N.   our pope,

N.   our bishop, with all bishops, priests, and deacons, and all your ho-ly people,

may we follow your paths in faith and hope and radiate our joy and trust to all the world.

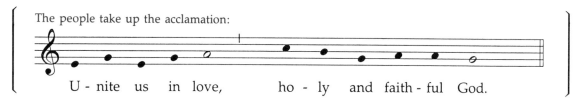

The people take up the acclamation:

U - nite us   in love,   ho - ly   and faith - ful God.

With hands extended, the priest continues the prayer on page 70.

III. JESUS, WAY TO THE FATHER

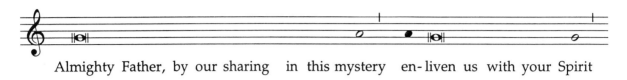

Almighty Father, by our sharing in this mystery en-liven us with your Spirit

and conform us to the image of your Son. Strengthen the bonds of our communion with

N.   our pope,   N.   our bishop,   with all bishops, priests, and deacons,

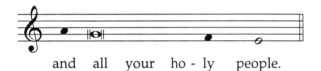

and   all   your   ho - ly   people.

The people take up the acclamation:

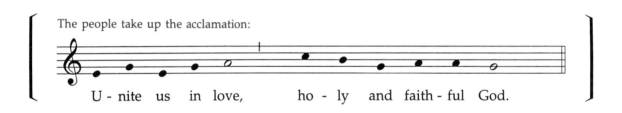

U - nite us   in love,   ho - ly   and faith - ful God.

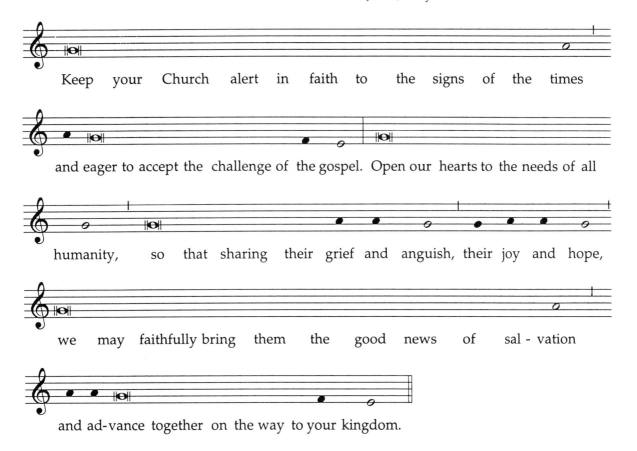

Keep your Church alert in faith to the signs of the times

and eager to accept the challenge of the gospel. Open our hearts to the needs of all

humanity, so that sharing their grief and anguish, their joy and hope,

we may faithfully bring them the good news of sal - vation

and ad-vance together on the way to your kingdom.

The people take up the acclamation:

U - nite us in love, ho - ly and faith - ful God.

With hands extended, the priest continues the prayer on page 70.

IV. JESUS, THE COMPASSION OF GOD

Lord, perfect your Church in faith and love   together with N. our pope,

N. our bishop,   with all bishops,   priests,   and   deacons,

and all those your Son has gained for you.

The people take up the acclamation:

U - nite us in love,   ho - ly and faith - ful God.

Open our eyes to the needs of all;   inspire us with words and deeds

to comfort those who labor and are burdened; keep our service of others

faithful to the example and command of Christ.

The people take up the acclamation:

U - nite us in love,   ho - ly and faith - ful God.

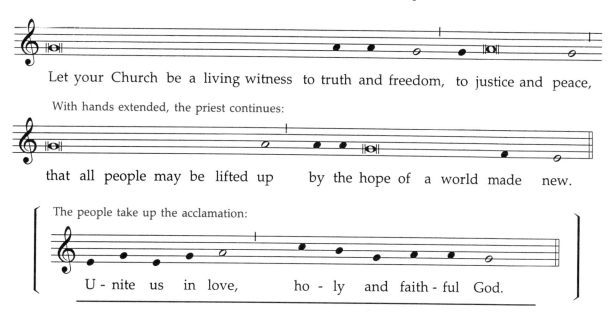

Let your Church be a living witness to truth and freedom, to justice and peace,

With hands extended, the priest continues:

that all people may be lifted up   by the hope of a world made   new.

The people take up the acclamation:

U - nite us   in love,   ho - ly   and faith - ful God.

With hands extended, the priest continues the prayer on page 70.

Be mindful of our brothers and sisters [N. and N.], who have fallen asleep in the

peace of Christ, and all the dead whose faith only you can know.

Lead them to the fullness of the resur - rection

and gladden them with the light of your face.

The people take up the acclamation:

U - nite us in love, ho - ly and faith - ful God.

When our pilgrimage on earth is complete, welcome us into your heavenly home,

where we shall dwell with you for ever. There, with Mary, the Virgin Mother of God,

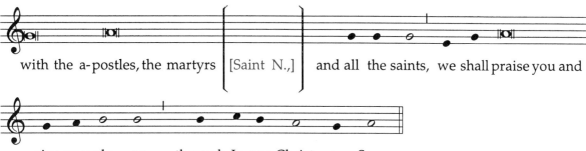

with the a-postles, the martyrs [Saint N.,] and all the saints, we shall praise you and give you glo - ry through Je-sus Christ, your Son.

He joins his hands.

He takes the chalice and the paten with the host and, lifting them up, sings:

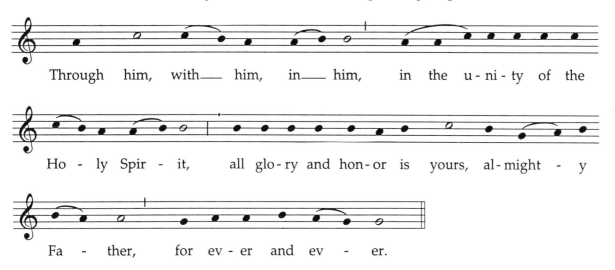

Through him, with— him, in— him, in the u - ni - ty of the Ho - ly Spir - it, all glo-ry and hon-or is yours, al-might - y Fa - ther, for ev - er and ev - er.

The people answer:

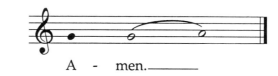

A - men.———

Or, in place of the single *Amen*, the following may be sung:

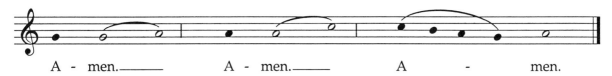

A - men.——— A - men.——— A - men.